LEAN

SIX-SIGMA

*A Step-by-Step Guide to
Measuring and Monitoring
Project Performance*

by **WALTER MC FASTER**

Congratulation on purchase this book and thank You for doing so.

Please enjoy*!*

Table of Contents

CHAPTER 01

Introduction to Lean

If you are someone who is an executive of a big firm, a micro startup company or even a housewife, a student or an entry level employee in any firm, Lean Six Sigma can make you most effective and the most successful in your respective field. Yes, you read that right, lean six sigma can be applied in every field, whether it is domestic or commercial, lean six sigma will help you achieve the maximum potential. Lean six sigma is the technique which has transformed the face of modern industrial landscape and has immensely added value in the businesses which apply this technique. The beauty of this technique is that it can be applied to any business and field regardless of the nature and size of the businesses in which it is applied. Lean six sigma does involve some mathematical calculations, but you don't have to worry about it.

In this book, lean six sigma will be explained to you in plain and simple terms. This book holds the key to your excellence and success in your respective field. The technique will be explained to you from scratch and it will be explained to you from everyday examples. Not only that, but you will be also trained to do simple calculations and analysis. This will not only allow you to understand this technique, but you will be also able to apply the lean six sigma in your required field and reap its benefits. This revolutionary technique will be elaborated to you in the best and most effective way. So, get ready to enhance your abilities to the highest possible level and become the best version of yourself. Keep your highlighters, mobile phones or pencils close so that you may underline the important stuff or make notes about your own thoughts on the topic.

So, without further ado, let's start discussing this revolutionary technique.

WHAT EXACTLY IS LEAN?

To understand the whole concept of lean six sigma, it is important to comprehend what do we mean by the term "lean".

Lean is a term very extensively used in nutrition and bodybuilding. A bodybuilder is said to be in a "lean" condition if he has very little or no body fat. His muscles are toned, and you can see every muscle fiber, which he took great effort to make, with great clarity and detail. In relation to the topic we are discussing, the essence of the meaning of "lean" is quite similar to that discussed in bodybuilding. But what we consider as unnecessary fat and the technique we apply to get rid of it through the lean six sigma philosophy is of totally another dimension. The nature of the word "lean" constitutes of various parameters we take to make a process efficient and in the lean six sigma technique, lean is the practical application of common sense in the smooth running of an organization.

Just as the bodybuilder who has removed any unnecessary body fat from his body and has become a structure of pure muscle, the "lean" focuses on reducing or removing all the unnecessary procedures or steps in a process.

Simply defined, "lean is the elimination of all forms of non-value-added work from the customer's perspective in business transactions and processes."

EXPLANATION OF LEAN PHILOSOPHY

If we look into the verbs or the action words involved or used in the above definition, we can expand the details of the lean philosophy from it quite comfortably. The first verb or action word used in the definition we stated of lean is "elimination". In fact, it is the most important and defining word of the lean philosophy. What we can deduct from the use of the word "elimination" in the definition of lean is that lean is actually a simplifying process. It is a philosophy which focuses on the removal of the unnecessary steps or procedures involved in a process. It should be noted that elimination of any process or procedure under the lean philosophy should not result in deterioration of quality of the product which the system produces. In other words, the process that is eliminated under the lean philosophy should be of no constructive consequences whatsoever. As this book is focused on educating the masses having little or no background of the lean philosophy, we will take everyday example of elimination of a step because of the lean philosophy.

Let us take the example of getting a pizza delivered to a customer's doorsteps using the lean philosophy. In a conventional setup, the customer calls the pizza place and orders the pizza he or she wants to have. For this, generally, the customer has to select a flavor, size of the pizza and tell if he or she needs any extra toppings of cheese, chicken or olives etc. The order might be placed under a minute if the customer who is calling is a regular at the place. However, the call might take too long if the person calling is a fresh customer who has never ordered the pizza from that particular pizza place. The customer might demand a flavor or size of the pizza which is simply not produced at that particular pizza place or the customer might have to ponder what exactly he or she has to order while the person receiving the order has to wait until the customer has finally made up his or her mind. Even if the customer is able to describe the pizza he or she wants, they still might take a while to tell the address where they want the pizza to be delivered. Such a situation might be very annoying for another customer who tries to call but his or her call is not connected to the pizza place as it is already busy with another customer. To keep the call short, the person dealing with the client might talk hastily to the new customer who might feel unwelcome because of the hasty tone. Also, there is a big chance that the new customer might place a wrong order if he or she isn't given proper time to think about what they really want to order. In short, calls are not a good means of deciding what to order especially if you are a new customer. And the lean philosophy dictates that this step should be removed from the process which involves placing an order. And if we take a closer look, many pizza places have implemented the lean philosophy in this specific instance. We now often come across pizza places who have made online mobile applications available for their customers where they can select the pizza, they want by choosing from various options which the pizza place provides. They can change their order at any time before they finally submit it and they can take all the time they want to decide what exactly they want to order. And there is no limit to the number of people ordering their pizza at a given instance. Hence, the elimination of calling to place an order, which was non-value-added work, under the philosophy of lean resulted in great improvement of the efficiency of the process of placing an order.

Now that we have grasped the idea that lean is an elimination process, the next logical step would be to determine what sort of procedures or steps are deemed as unnecessary and are supposed to be eliminated because of the lean philosophy. This information can also be deduced from the definition of lean that we mentioned earlier which stated that, "lean is the elimination of all forms of non-value-added work from the customer's perspective in business transactions and processes." In this definition of lean it is clearly stated that non-value-added work from the customer's perspective is the process which is deemed to be eliminated from the process. Non-value added can be any step which does not provide any benefit to the customer by adding something of value. If we take a look at the example of the elimination of calling to place an order of pizza because of the lean philosophy, we understand that it is actually the waiting time that has been eliminated from the ordering process. By introducing the mobile application, the waiting time to place an order has been removed. The time required to wait for the turn to place an order resulted in no value addition from the customer's perspective, so it was an unnecessary thing and its removal from the process was necessary under the lean philosophy. This might appear to be common sense now, but it took a century after the industrial revolution for the executives of big companies to realize that waiting for the turn to place an order is unnecessary and should not be faced by the customers. Even today, many establishments consider the waiting of the customers to place their orders as a matter of pride which shows the importance of their company, whereas in reality it is a big drawback and the customer may switch if he or she is able to get a company which provides similar quality product with no time required to wait before placing the order.

Another important aspect of the lean philosophy is that it is customer oriented. It means that a step or procedure is deemed to be eliminated only by keeping the customer's perspective in mind. Perhaps waiting for placing the order might make you feel good about your company and your competitors might get jealous by looking at the long queues of customers outside your door. But perhaps it is the long queue which is holding back many customers to come and order. So, it is advised in the lean philosophy that you always look at the process from the customer's perspective.

SALIENT FEATURES OF LEAN

After the above discussion, we can conclude that lean is:

A philosophy which focuses on the removal of the unnecessary steps or procedures involved in a process.

It is customer-oriented and the steps which need to be eliminated are determined based on the customer's perspective.

It is focused on the business transactions, but this philosophy can be easily implemented in our daily lives to get maximum amount of efficiency out of it.

Details about the lean philosophy and how it is implemented in business to enhance your effectiveness will be shared with you in the entailing pages of this book.

CHAPTER 07

Introduction to Six Sigma

THE SIX SIGMA PHILOSOPHY

Sigma is actually a symbol to denote the standard deviation of a population. Standard deviation is a measure to quantify the variation of a set of samples from their average value. These concepts are basically from the subject of statistics. Before defining what exactly six sigma is, it is important to understand the basic concepts of mean and standard deviation as well as upper and lower specification limits. Because the philosophy of six sigma can't be grasped properly without having clear understanding of mean, standard deviation and their effects on the level of variations.

These concepts are mathematical in nature, but we will make sure that the explanation of these concepts is based on the examples of pizzas, in which people are always interested, so that the topic doesn't become dull and monotonous.

MEAN

Mean is the average of all the values of a set of samples. It is calculated by summing up all the values of the samples available and dividing the sum by the number of samples. Generally, mean represents the value which is generally expected from the values taken from the available samples.

Let us take an example from a hypothetical pizza shop and let us assume that the name of the pizza place is "Sigma Six Pizzas". Sigma Six Pizzas focus on home delivery and take-away as their shop is very small and they don't have a proper dining hall. But as their pizza is one of the best in town, thanks to the precise technique they use in baking, they have a healthy customer base and their home delivery orders are very high in numbers. One of the reasons of the high numbers of orders is that the management of the Six Sigma Pizzas offer no charges against your order if the delivery is not made within forty minutes after you have placed your order. On a certain Monday, the business remained slow, but they still managed to get 50 pizzas delivered and get 30 orders. The details of the delivery of those pizzas are enlisted in the following table.

Delivery #	# of Pizzas	Delivery Time	Diff. from Average Delivery Time
1	3	20	0.8667
2	2	20	0.8667
3	1	18	-1.1333
4	3	20	0.8667
5	3	20	0.8667
6	3	20	0.8667
7	1	18	-1.1333
8	1	18	-1.1333
9	1	18	-1.1333
10	1	18	-1.1333

11	1	18	-1.1333
12	1	18	-1.1333
13	1	18	-1.1333
14	2	20	0.8667
15	2	20	0.8667
16	2	20	0.8667
17	2	20	0.8667
18	2	20	0.8667
19	3	22	2.8667
20	1	18	-1.1333
21	2	20	0.8667
22	2	20	0.8667
23	2	20	0.8667
24	3	20	0.8667

25	1	18	-1.1333
26	1	18	-1.1333
27	1	18	-1.1333
28	1	18	-1.1333
29	1	18	-1.1333
30	2	20	0.8667

Now, if we would want to calculate the mean or average of the time taken to deliver the order, it will come out to be 19.1333 minutes

STANDARD DEVIATION

Standard deviation holds the most important place in the six sigma philosophy. As it is clear from the fact that sigma (σ) is the symbol used to denote the standard deviation of a set of samples. It is defined as a quantity expressing by how much the members of a group differ from the mean value for the group. If the value of standard deviation is small, then it means that variation in the values of the samples available is small. If the standard deviation is of a higher value, then the values of the samples will be relatively dispersed.

Standard deviation of any given set of samples can be easily calculated by summing up difference between each value from the mean value and dividing the result by the total number of values. In other words, standard deviation is the average difference between the values and their mean. However, as the difference can be negative as well as positive, so the sum of the values might cancel each other's effect and we may not be able to get the accurate picture of the dispersion of the values through the standard deviation. To avoid the cancellation, all differences are squared so that the values are always positive before adding them. The effect of taking the square is cancelled by taking the square root of the value after the summation. Mathematically, the formula for standard deviation is as follows:

$$s = \sqrt{\frac{\sum_{i=1}^{N}(x_i - \overline{x})^2}{N - 1}}$$

Now, let us calculate the standard deviation of our hypothetical pizza place "Six Sigma Pizzas". After all, mathematics can only be understood by its application rather than by expressing it with the help of confusing formulas.

So, our calculations suggest that the standard deviation of the "Six Sigma Pizzas" is just 1.136 minutes with respect to their mean value of 19.133 minutes. Which is way below than forty minutes. No wonder the company is so confident about their delivery period that they have offered free pizzas in case they fail to deliver them in time. This, of course, enhances the confidence of the customers in the service of the pizza place that they will never be left hungry for too long if they order a pizza from Six Sigma Pizzas.

UPPER SPECIFICATION LIMIT

If you are a person who does not like spicy food much, then perhaps you will not appreciate a pizza place which adds a little too much of red chilli in your pizza, especially if you told them not to. Of course you will prefer a pizza which has a light sprinkle of spices all over it instead of a plain, bland one. The exact level beyond which you will reject the pizza and consider it too spicy will be considered as your upper specification limit. The value of upper specification limit can be of quantity, as in our example, length, color etc., depending on the parameter it defines. For example, a certain length of a shirt might be the upper specification limit for you and if the shirt is longer than that limit then you will reject it and consider it faulty. Also, if a customer has ordered a shirt in a certain shade of blue and if the shirt is colored darker than the color specified, its upper specification limit, then the customer will reject the shirt as it is beyond the upper specification limit.

In plain words, upper specification limit is the value beyond which the product is considered as faulty.

LOWER SPECIFICATION LIMIT

Let us consider the example of the pizza that we took in defining the upper specification limit. As we assumed that although you like your pizza to be a little less spicy, you don't want it to be totally devoid of the spices. If the pizza has the spices below the level you would like it to be, you will toss the pizza away and reject it. So, in this instance, the minimum level of spices which is acceptable to you will be your lower specification limit. Same as in the case of upper specification limit, the value of lower specification limit can be of quantity, as in our example, length, color etc., depending on the parameter it defines. For example, a certain length of a shirt might be the lower specification limit for you and if the shirt is shorter than that limit then you will reject it and consider it faulty. Also, if a customer has ordered a shirt in a certain shade of blue and if the shirt is colored lighter than the color specified, its lower specification limit, then the customer will reject the shirt as it is below the lower specification limit.

In plain words, lower specification limit is the value below which the product is considered as faulty.

WHAT EXACTLY IS SIX SIGMA?

Now that you are well acquainted with the meaning of mean, standard deviation, lower specification limit and upper specification limit, understanding six sigma philosophy is no problem for you anymore. Let us consider our hypothetical pizza place, the Six Sigma Pizzas. As you have seen from the data of delivery time from a particular day, you might have noticed that some time periods for delivering the pizza were greater than simply adding one standard deviation time in the average time. However, it is quite clear that in most of the scenarios, the delivery time is in the range of the average value plus/minus one standard deviation. But, as you know, Six Sigma Pizzas offers that you will not have to pay for the pizza if the delivery is not made in time. So even a few orders, if delivered late, can result in a substantial amount of loss. Therefore, the company has to make sure that all orders can be delivered in time to by reducing the variations in the time of delivery in order to avoid wastage. And this is where the six sigma philosophy comes in play. It focuses on reducing the defects to such a level that they are measured in terms of defects per million opportunities (DPMO) instead of defects in terms of percentage. Attaining such a low level of defect rate is only possible if almost all of the produce is under the range of the upper specification limit and above the lower specification limit. If the upper and lower specification limits are greater than the value we get by adding or subtracting six standard deviations (six sigma values) from the mean, then it is said that the company or organization has achieved 6 sigma level.

Simply defined, it is a statistically based methodology used to reduce variations and remove defects in various processes and business transactions.

CHAPTER 08

Evolution of Lean and Six Sigma

Now that you have been introduced with lean six sigma philosophy, a little background knowledge about its progress and evolution will enhance your understanding on this subject. Generally, most books start by focusing on the evolution phase and give a detailed history of the topic before delving into the details, but in case of technical topics, such as the one we are exploring, it is better to get a basic know how of what you are studying and its benefits. In this way, you may become more eager to get more deeply involved in the topic once you understand its significance in the introductory chapter.

Lean six sigma is a combination of two techniques and philosophies which evolved separately and merged with each other at the very beginning of the twenty-first century.

EVOLUTION OF LEAN THINKING

Lean is indeed a form of application of common sense in business management. Its roots go way back in the era of industrial revolution.

FREDRICK TAYLOR

In around the last decade of the nineteenth century, Fredrick Taylor, a dynamic management consultant applied scientific methods to determine best practices and do extensive time studies. Fredrick Taylor was a mechanical engineering professional and is considered to be the father of scientific management. Before Taylor, every craftsman had his own methodology and collaboration of many craftsmen to produce something in bulk quantity was not common. Even in mega projects, no best and most effective and efficient method was defined. Fredrick Taylor was one of the pioneers in applying scientific research and methodology in industrial management.

HENRY FORD

Henry Ford is one of the most iconic founders of car manufacturing companies. He is responsible for steering American Auto Industry to unprecedented heights. When he introduced the model-t, it was nothing short of an industrial revolution in itself. Model-t changed the way people travel once and for all, it is the model which made cars to be used on an unprecedented level popularity among the masses.

He pioneered the first manufacturing strategy which was comprehensive in all aspects and which enhanced the production capacity and efficiency to the levels which were thought to be unattainable in the past. The concept and application of flow production, which was the lean approach applied by Ford, made production simplified by placing the fabrication equipment in a sequenced process made production rate very high. This seems quite common sense, but back then the idea was nothing short of a revelation and it made all the difference.

TAIICHI OHNO

Fredrick Taylor and Henry Ford might be the forerunners of lean management, but it was Taiichi Ohno who introduced lean management to the world in the 1960's. He was a Japanese businessman and an assembly manager of Toyota. He is considered to be the father of lean management on the basis of his work done in the Toyota manufacturing plant in the United States of America which was the first production plant to apply this philosophy on an industrial scale.

The production plant of Toyota where Mr. Ohno worked was huge, he realized the importance of inventory management in the production operations. Inventory is basically the goods or parts present in the factory, of course, as time passes some items become less in quantity and the stock needs to be replenished. Inventory management focuses on maintaining the stock as it is consumed. Taiichi Ohno worked on efficiently maintaining the stock, introducing the philosophy of "just in time ". Just in time (JIT), makes sure that the stock present in the facility is neither surplus nor less than required but it is at the optimal level.

He is also responsible for pointing out the seven essential wastes which need to be eliminated so that lean manufacturing can be attained, and profitability of the manufacturing operation can be enhanced. All of these concepts are very essential and constitute the foundation of lean, hence we will discuss them in more detail in the entailing chapter.

Evolution of the Six Sigma Approach

As discussed previously, six sigma is a statistically based methodology used to reduce variations and remove defects in various processes and business transactions. It is a relatively newer approach in doing business and increasing its profitability. The basic reason behind the late application of such an effective methodology in business is perhaps the fact that standardization was not common among various products for a long time in the past. But in the first quarter of the twentieth century, statistical approach was first taken as a potential tool to help enhance businesses and production. Walter Shewhart may be crowned as the pioneer in applying statistics in this field.

WALTER SHEWHART

Walter Shewhart can be classified as a modern polymath. He was an engineer, a physicist and a statistician. He was from the United States of America. He is crowned by many as father of statistical quality control because of his pioneering and extensive work in this field in the 1920's. He is responsible for introducing the control charts and elaborating the difference between special and common cause variables and how they contribute as a problem in a certain process. Walter Shewhart's work can be considered as a precursor to the six sigma philosophy.

BILL SMITH

Bill Smith is credited with introducing the six sigma approach for the first time while he was working in the company Motorola in the mid 1980's. He is rightly crowned as the father of six sigma. He was an engineer and belonged to the United States of America. Six sigma is a process which helps to minimize wastes by reducing variations in the process and hence reducing the number of defects in the production operations.

JACK WELCH

If Bill Smith was the father of six sigma then Jack Welch is definitely the Godfather of this approach. Jack Welch nurtured the six sigma thinking and made it a main stream philosophy when he applied it at General Electric and made it its central strategy in the mid 1990's. Mr. Jack Welch was the chief executive officer (C.E.O.) as well as Chairman of General Electric when he introduced this concept in the company. He is said to have admitted that six sigma is the biggest and most important initiative ever taken at General Electric.

CHAPTER 09

Methodology of Lean and Six Sigma

As defined in the very beginning, lean is "elimination of all forms of non-value-added work from the customer's perspective in business transactions and processes."

LEAN METHODOLOGY

When we look at any business or process, different operations are the building blocks of them which combine to form that business or process. Some operations add value, and some do not. So, it is important to understand the concept of value from the customer's perspective so that lean can be applied successfully. The operations can be categorized according to the value they produce from the customer's perspective as follows.

BUSINESS NON-VALUE ADD ACTIVITIES

The operations or activities which do not result in any value addition or produce any beneficial outcome but are still necessary for running the company or organization are termed as business non-value add activities.

The most common example of it are the operations which must be carried out to achieve the regulatory requirements imposed by the government. These are generally the tasks which do not add any value from the customer's point of view but they still can't be eliminated.

ESSENTIAL ACTIVITIES

These are the operations, tasks and activities which produce valuable outcome from the customer's perspective and the customer is willing to pay for it.

WASTES

The activities or operations which do not produce any beneficial outcome or result in value addition from the customer's perspective are termed as waste in the lean philosophy.

In a typical business process, more than eighty percent of the activities can be classified as wastes or non-value add activities. This is indeed a tremendous amount of activity which produce nothing. The proportion also signifies that one can achieve extraordinary edge over average businesses just by limiting or eliminating the non-value add activities. When you are able to control the amount of waste activities, you will be able to increase the proportion of activities for which the customer is actually willing to pay for. And this will make all the difference between your extraordinary efficient and profitable company against the average runt of the litter company.

This calls for an increased scrutinization of the processes so that waste can be identified. After many years of efforts in finding various types of wastes, experts have boiled down their analysis of waste and found them to be of the following seven types.

Motion

Transportation

Waiting

Overproduction

Inventory

Over processing

Rework

MOTION

It is the movement of the employee who is performing a certain operation. If an operation involves a lot of movement on behalf of the employee, it produces no such feature for which the customer is interested in paying, hence it is classified as a waste. Examples of such waste is going to different offices, going to the printer, searching for any missing information.

TRANSPORTATION

This might come as unexpected to you, but any conveyance of a product is considered waste. Assembly lines, shipping or mailing move a product from one place to another, but they do not add any value to it. Transportation really does not transform or change a product; all it does is move that product from one place to another. Amazon is the company which has tremendously gained by curtailing this waste by building warehouses all across the United States of America. This greatly reduced the need of transportation to deliver the product to the customer which resulted in extraordinary profit for the company.

WAITING

This is perhaps the most common form of waste in almost all fields all over the globe. Delay in the process or improper flow of the procedure result in waiting. Most common examples of waiting that the customer has to endure are waiting for clarification, delivery of the order and waiting to finalize the deal.

OVERPRODUCTION

Overproduction is the waste which is a result of producing the goods or services in quantities which are higher than the demand for them. Overproduction generally happens when the planned production rate is based on forecast of the sales rather than the present market demand.

INVENTORY

Any type of service or supply, raw materials etc., which is kept in quantities higher than the minimum required to produce the product and get the job done can be termed as inventory. Inventory is something which also ties up the resources of the company as well as takes up space and demand special facilities in some cases. Too much inventory also results in unnecessary motion as well as transportation, in other words, it is a non-value-added activity which produces other types of wastes as well.

OVER PROCESSING

In many instances of producing a product, extra work is done which the customer is not interested in paying for. This type of work involves expenses but does not give any profit or revenues in return. If the product is made extra shiny but the customer is not affected about whether the product is shiny or not, then shining that product may be categorized as a waste because of over processing. Of course, if the customer does care about whether the product is shiny or not, then shining the product should be classified as an essential activity rather than over processing, in the end it all boils down to the customer's perspective.

REWORK

Any modifications or improvements in the product which are done in the product after its final step of manufacturing is termed as rework and is classified as a waste in the lean philosophy. Because lean stresses on doing the right thing the first time, if a product is not defective then it will not need any rework, hence rework is an additional step which can be avoided without affecting the quality or standard of the product.

LEAN TOOLS

Many techniques and simple creative thinking is done to develop tools which help make the process and business lean. Lean tools, basically, are just a practical application of common sense in business management to make it more impactful, efficient and profitable.

Some tools of lean are enlisted below.

The 5S

Mistake-proofing

Kanban

SMED

Andon

Bottleneck analysis

Continuous flow

Muda (waste)

Root cause analysis

SMART goals

Jidoka

KPI

Production leveling

Gamba

Detailed description and analysis of the tools used in the lean methodology might require a separate book of its own, however, a brief discussion on some of the most important and extensively used tools of lean is done in the proceeding paragraphs.

THE 5S

The 5S is basically a workplace organization tool. The 5S which constitute the following steps.

Sort
Set in order
Shine
Standardize
Sustain
Hoshim Kanri

These are the guiding principles which, if followed, result in an efficient work environment.

MISTAKE-PROOFING

Mistake proofing is known as po-ka yo-ke in Japanese. It is a design approach which makes it impossible for a mistake to occur or once a mistake or error occurs, it becomes obvious right away. Example of po-ka yo-ke is the plug and socket having different shapes of each hole of the socket and leg of the switch so that they can be connected in a specific order.

KANBAN

It is the lean approach developed by the pioneers of lean, Taiichi Ohno. The name, Kanban, is taken because of the cards used in this methodology. It is an inventory management approach focusing on the Just in Time (JIT) principle which Mr. Ohno introduced in the Toyota factory where he worked.

SMED (Single Minute Exchange of Dies)

It is a technique applied to significantly lower the time required to complete the change of equipment. SMED, short for single minute change of dies, focuses on converting as many steps of Chang over of equipment to "external" as possible. So that the process may continue while the changeover of the equipment is done. This approach streamlines the workflow and reduces downtime.

Andon

It's a management term which refers to the system to notify management, maintenance and other processes of quality and process problems. The workstation has an alert to indicate if a problem arises, it can be activated by a worker or by an automatic system. It informs the system that it may include some issues which should be resolved. The whole system is stopped so the issue can be corrected. It brings the immediate attention to the problem so that it can be resolved.

BOTTLENECK ANALYSIS

A bottleneck refers to a process that causes the system to stop or delay the outcome of the system, a process that takes the longest cycle time. Bottleneck analysis should be done when the expansion of capacity is being planned. Only increasing the capacity of the other processes will not increase the overall output as they will still be limi2by bottleneck processes. Bottleneck analysis identify which steps of the process limit the overall throughput and improve it. It improves the performance by finding the weakest part in manufacturing process and strengthen it.

CONTINUOUS FLOW

Continuous flow is the movement of the product or service through the production process to finish without hindrance. In an efficient continuous flow, the cycle time is equal to the lead time. Continuous flow can reduce the wastage of time when done properly and can significantly reduce cost. It lowers the inventory level. It improves the on time delivery as there is no waste or unwanted goods piled up and only the right goods are move forward through the system. It delivers high quality products as mistakes in continuous flow only affect one part of the process.

MUDA(WASTE)

Muda is anything in the process that do not add value from the customer's perspective and the customers are not willing to pay for it. The primary goal of lean manufacturing is to eliminate the waste.

ROOT CALL ANALYSIS

It is a methodology to solve problems that begin by solving the problems related to the core of the system rather than fixing the problems on the surface which only give temporary solution.

SMART GOALS

SMART goals are the goals that are: specific, measurable, attainable, relevant and time specific. It helps to achieve the goals.

JIDOKA (AUTONOMATION)

Autonomation is described as intelligent automation or automation with a human touch. This type of automation advise some supervisory functions instead of production functions. This means that if an abnormal situation occurs then the machine is stopped and workers stop the production line. And for this the Jidoka follows the steps of first detection of the abnormality, stop the process, fix or correct the immediate condition and find the root cause of the problem and install a countermeasure. Autonomation prevents overproduction, over inventory and elimination of the waste and focus on solving problems and make sure they don't occur again.

KPI (KEY PERFORMANCE INDICATOR)

The key performance indicator indicates how well the company is performing and effectively working towards the achievement of its goals. Organizations use key performance indicators at different levels to evaluate their success possibilities. High level KPI refers to the performance of the overall organization and low level KPI refers to the processes of the departments.

PRODUCTION LEVELING

Production leveling is also known as production smoothing oor in Japanese the original term as "heijunka" is a technique used to reduce waste. The goal is to produce a goods at a constant rate so that the further processing can be done at a constant and predictable rate. It reduces the lead time and inventory by keeping the batches smaller.

GEMBA

The term gemba refers to the personal observation of the work- where the work is happening. Gemba is derived from a Japanese word *gembutsu,* which means "real thing". Or sometimes it refers to "real place". Observation in-person, the core principle of the tool, observe where the work is done, interacting with the people and the process for the change.

HOSHIN KANRI (POLICY DEPLOYMENT)

It is a process that identifies the business critical needs and demands and develop the capabilities of the employees, achieved by the alignment of company's resources at all levels. Policy deployment increases the efficiency of the business. It focuses on achieving the company's goals by meeting the demands of the customers, employees, shareholders, suppliers and the environment. Policy deployment is an ideal report structure.

VALUE STREAM MAPPING

Value stream mapping is an amazing tool which helps to identify major non-value add activities (wastes), which must be removed from the process to make it lean.

WHAT DO WE MEAN BY A VALUE STREAM MAP?

A value stream map is a graphical representation of all the activities which constitute any process under consideration. The activities represented in the value stream map can be essential activities, wastes or non-value add business activities.

It contains a lot of information regarding the process under consideration and is extremely helpful in understanding the flow of the procedure.

WHAT DO WE GET BY DRAWING A VALUE STREAM MAP?

When a value stream map is constructed, understanding of the mechanism of the flow of activities and their significance becomes clear to the management and anyone studying the value stream map. It also helps to identify the nonessential steps in the process which must eliminated from the process to make it lean.

TIPS FOR DEVELOPING A VALUE STREAM MAP

Value stream map is a simple tool for making the business lean. If applied efficiently, it can result in great value generation with minimal investment of time, mental capabilities and physical efforts.

Some of the tips that might come in handy when you are developing a value stream map for your organization are discussed with you in the entailing paragraphs.

USE STICKY NOTES

Sticky notes are fun to work with, but that is not their main appeal or attractive feature. You can comfortably make changes in them and you can color code them as well. For instance, you can designate green colored sticky notes only to be used for essential activities, red sticky notes for wastes, and grey colored sticky notes for non-value add business activities. This way, it becomes easy to identify the different types of activities when the value stream map is studied.

MAKE SURE THAT YOUR WORKSTATION IS SPACIOUS

When developing a value stream map, things can become very messy very fast. If you are working on a value stream map in a congested space, it will become very difficult to avoid cluttering up different things. The more spacious the workstation is, the easier it will be to manage it. It would be much preferable if you work on a big white board or a giant desk when you are developing a value stream map.

DON'T DEVELOP THE VALUE STREAM MAP ALL ALONE

It is best to develop the value stream map with a team of professionals who are personally involved in the process. It eliminates or reduces the possibility of overlooking a step or classifying an essential activity as a waste or vice versa. It also allows you to have an eagle's view of all the steps involved in the process and find the loopholes in the process.

SIX SIGMA METHODOLOGY

As mentioned earlier, "Six Sigma is a statistical based methodology used to reduce variations and remove defects in various processes and business transactions."

We have already discussed the pertinent concepts of six sigma such as standard deviation, mean, upper specification limit and lower specification limit so we will not repeat those here. However, a concise discussion of variations must be done to continue the topic in an orderly fashion, so it is discussed here under.

WHAT EXACTLY ARE VARIATIONS?

Variations is actually the amount of difference between the statistical mean of the sample and the various points which are used to calculate the mean in the first place. In simpler terms, it is the magnitude with which the performance of any system varies from its average value.

In the six sigma approach, variation is simply calculated by finding the standard deviation of the sample. Standard deviation, as you remember, is a concept which has been discussed previously so we will not repeat it again over here. However, here is the formula through which standard deviation is calculated.

WHAT ACTUALLY ARE DEFECTS?

If we analyze the definition of six sigma, controlling the variations is the action that we undertake, and reduction of defects is the outcome that we would like to achieve through this action. This calls for a good understanding of the concepts of both variations as well as defects.

When it comes to the concept of a defect, we can say that a defect is some product, or a service provided to the customer which does not meet the clearly defined requirements of the customer. In simpler terms, it is any process outcome which outside of the defined specifications.

In six sigma, we generally analyze or calculate defects in terms of DPU which stands for Defects Per Unit or DPMO which stands for Defects Per Million Opportunities and is calculated as follows.

$$Defects\,Per\,Unit\,(DPMO) = \frac{Defects\,per\,Unit \times 1,000,000}{Opportunities\,per\,Unit}$$

Now that you have got yourself well acquainted with the concepts of six sigma, let us observe the extraordinary difference between various sigma levels. As you know that sigma is basically the standard deviation. As we improve from one sigma level to another, it will mean that we have achieved defect-free production up-to that level of standard deviation. For example, a sigma four process will signify that all products which are under four standard deviation away from the average value are defect-free. We will enhance our sigma level as we reduce the standard deviation of the process by reducing variations and hence more proportion of the output will become defect-free. As we enhance our sigma level, the Defects Per Million Opportunities will decrease automatically. To get a hold of this concept, different sigma levels along with their corresponding Defects Per Million Opportunities as well as the corresponding defect-free outcomes in percentage are enlisted in the table below.

Sigma Level	DPMO	% Defect-free
2	308,538	69
3	66,807	93.3
4	6,210	99.38
5	233	99.977
6	3	99.9997

SIGNIFICANCE OF THE SIGMA LEVELS

A thought might come across your mind when you study the above table, that according to it, we are able to achieve 99% defect-free production when we advance from sigma three level to sigma four level. Of course, 99% is really an appealing number. But when it comes to critical services involving life and death situations, 99% precision is simply not good enough.

To understand the implications of the six sigma level, let us observe the example of surgical procedures. In this case, 99% successful surgical operations will mean that roughly 5000 people will die on the surgery table because of an unsuccessful procedure, whereas this number trickles down to just 2 persons losing their lives while undergoing a surgery. Of course, the death of two human beings is still a tragic loss but it is way better than losing 5000 patients a week.

In the modern world, every human being has to perform more than one financial transaction every day on a regular basis. If banks and other financial institutions are able to achieve 99% defect-free outcomes, we will still be left with a staggering number of roughly 150,000 incorrect financial transactions per hour, this number is reduced to about 75 mistakes per hour if the financial sector achieve the six sigma level.

When it comes to travelling, air travel is the safest mode of transportation. But had the airlines satisfied by 99% error free flights, we will be faced with about 6 fatal accidents per day, whereas the number of fatal accidents become about 1 per year when the airlines get to six sigma level.

Concepts and Tools of Six Sigma

Apart from calculating the mean, standard deviation, determining the upper specification limit and lower specification limit and finding the defects per million opportunities (DPMO), many handy tools are developed and utilized to reduce variations and minimize defects. These tools and techniques are termed as six sigma tools and some of them are listed hereunder.

Fishbone Diagram

Why-Why-Why Diagram

Pareto Diagram

Correlation Chart

Punchlist

Failure Mode Analysis

Zero Defect

Detailed description and analysis of the tools used in the six sigma methodology might require a separate book of its own, however, a brief discussion on some of the most important and extensively used tools of six sigma is done in the proceeding paragraphs.

PARETO DIAGRAM

It is a simple bar chart in which the bars are ranked in decreasing order of occurrence. Pareto diagram comes in handy for identifying the major contributors of defects and variations. Vilfredo Pareto was an Italian economist and sociologist who made a critical observation that in almost all aspects, close to 80% of the product is produced by almost 20% of the producers and the remaining 20% is produced by the 80% of the producers. Pareto diagram helps us identify the small proportion of the troublemakers which cause the majority of the damage in a process.

WHY-WHY-WHY DIAGRAM

It is a tree diagram. The Why-Why-Why diagram is developed in a manner that a child statement is formed by asking "why" the parent problem occurred. It is much similar to the cause-and-effect diagram. It is a great tool for brainstorming and reaching the root cause of the defects and variations in a particular process.

FISHBONE DIAGRAM

Kauro Ishikawa developed the Fishbone diagram which is also known by the name of Ishikawa diagram. It gets its name, Fishbone, because of its visual resemblance to a fish's skeleton. Where major causes of a particular event have further branches comprising of the causes which develop the major contributor of the problem in the first place.

CHAPTER 10

The Lean Six Sigma Philosophy

Lean six sigma is the practical application of the lean philosophy and the six sigma philosophy in running a business. It is the result of years of professionalism and evolution in the business management so that maximum customer satisfaction can be achieved by applying minimum resources, making huge profits for the company and producing great value for the customer. Before the year 2000, lean and six sigma had separate teams which focused on these philosophies separately, but it was soon realized that the goal of both of these techniques is same and hence they were taken as a singular philosophy known as lean six sigma. It is the result of lean six sigma technique that today some companies, such as Amazon, are able to guarantee same day delivery of the order placed by customers in many cities. It is indeed the combination of technology and lean six sigma management that broiler chicken is grown at an unprecedented rate, producing meat which is healthy and affordable for the masses. The successful application of lean six sigma in the businesses across the globe has transformed the market and increased productivity to new heights.

Lean six sigma philosophy focuses on removing any unnecessary steps which do not produce any beneficial outcomes for the customer and also makes sure that the product which is produced has minimum variations and maximum number of times, the product is not defective. This aspect of the philosophy results in reduced wastage and earns great profit for the vendor, making the business economically viable and fruitful.

Simply defined, lean six sigma is a business management approach which is utilized to enhance business processes and it is based on different tools of Lean and Six Sigma.

BENEFITS OF APPLYING LEAN SIX SIGMA

The benefits of applying the lean six sigma technique in management of businesses are proven and in large quantities. It is because of lean six sigma that customers are able to enjoy great quality of services and businesses are able to make unprecedented level of profits. In the fast changing and highly competitive world of the present day and age, lean six sigma has perhaps become a necessity rather than an extra positive feature for companies.

Some of the benefits of lean six sigma are as follows.

FASTER PROCESSES

By reducing or eliminating the seven types of wastes, the processes becomes increasingly efficient and fast. In fact, about 80 percent of the time required to complete a certain process can be eliminated by removing such wastes, making the process many times faster.

HIGHER QUALITY

As the variations in the product being produced are narrowed down, quality and precision of the outcomes is enhanced which helps in developing the brand of the organization which is applying lean six sigma. The stability of the process as a result of applying lean six sigma in the management of the business also results in an enhanced product quality.

HIGHER CUSTOMER SATISFACTION

Since customer is the main focus in the lean six sigma philosophy when it comes to determining value of the product, customer satisfaction goes through the roof when lean six sigma is applied. Because every aspect of the business becomes customer-oriented, the demands and needs of the customer are satisfied which makes the customer stick to the company and develop chances of future business opportunities.

INCREASED PROFITABILITY

All business activities are conducted to generate wealth, ultimately, the goal of lean six sigma is no different as well. Lean six sigma has proven to generate extraordinary amount of profits for the companies which implement it, either by increased sales or by enhancing the profit margin. It is the capacity of generating revenues and profits which has made lean six sigma philosophy so successful and popular among all successful organizations.

ENHANCED EMPLOYEE SATISFACTION

By engaging the employees in making improvements in the organization, lean six sigma incorporates a sense of being valued at the organization among its employees. Lean six sigma makes the employees stakeholders in the success of the organization and hence they become more attached and concerned with the company they serve in.

THE DMAIC CYCLE

It is Lean Six Sigma approach to minimize variations and defects and remove wastes in a process. It is employed to improve the preexisting process. DMAIC is the abbreviation for different steps of this cycle namely.

Define

Measure

Analyze

Improve

Control

DEFINE

Before jumping into a situation or a problem, it is important to understand and determine how the process of improvement should and would be conducted. Before you have completed the procedures involved in this step this, you cannot proceed to the any step of the DMAIC cycle. In this step, the project which is about to be improved is defined and its certain parameters are recognized. The key performance indicators (KPIs), which quantify the performance of the process, are set. Stakeholders in the project and various roles which every individual involved in the DMAIC cycle has to adopt are laid out clearly.

MEASURE

The current situation and performance of the process is measured after everything is defined in the DMAIC cycle. Value stream map, which has been discussed with you previously, is drawn to get a graphical representation of all the steps involved in the process. Relevant data is collected, and various functions are monitored. The capabilities of the current employees and equipment is assessed, and the baseline performance of the company is evaluated on the basis of this information.

ANALYZE

After the baseline performance of the process is measured, the next step of the DMAIC cycle is to analyze the situation and determine the root cause of the defects or inefficiency of the process. For this purpose, various tools such as the Fishbone Diagram are utilized. At the end of this analysis, we are able to develop a list of potential causes of the problems which should be reduced or eliminated in order to make the process lean and achieve six sigma level.

IMPROVE

After thorough analysis of the situation, we are able to get a list of troublemakers that need to be amended. For this purpose, a collective effort of all stakeholders is essential for the success. Brainstorming of new ideas and approach is quite simple but effective technique for improving the faulty process. A tentative value stream map should be drawn so that the necessary changes in the process and their implications can be observed and understood and decisions can be made about whether or not to proceed with the actions.

CONTROL

After improvements are finalized, it is essential to maintain and sustain the positive outcomes to harness the maximum potential of the DMAIC procedure. For this purpose, key performance indicators should be noted, updated, forecasted and given due importance. A control plan of sustaining the gains is made and the cycle is repeated over and over again so that constant improvements and increased productivity may achieved of the process on which DMAIC cycle is being applied.

KEY PLAYERS INVOLVED IN LEAN SIX SIGMA

To make lean six sigma a successful transformational agent, different individuals have to collaborate and work within a certain framework performing different type of tasks in relation to the role they are being assigned. Some of the key players involved in implementing the lean six sigma philosophy are as under.

Sponsor

Champion

Black or Green Belt

Process Owner

Team Members

A slight explanation of their roles in implementing the lean six sigma philosophy is discussed in the entailing paragraphs.

SPONSOR

It is the focal person running the six sigma procedures and operations and is responsible for providing all sorts of material required such as money, hardware, manpower etc. A sponsor is a person whose active participation is very essential for applying lean six sigma successfully in the culture of the organization.

CHAMPION

Champion is the person who spearheads the lean six sigma process and applies the changes in the company so that it may become lean and the product of the company may have least amount of variations and it is able to achieve the six sigma level. If there are some issues in the implementation of lean six sigma, champion is the individual responsible for removing it.

BLACK OR GREEN BELT

Black or Green Belt are the experts of the lean six sigma philosophy. They provide concrete solutions to the process owner for improving the efficiency of his or her organization. They assume the role of leaders and mentors to the team members of the lean six sigma team so that they can collect relevant information about the performance of the company and its various functions.

PROCESS OWNERS

Process owners have the highest stake in the success of the lean six sigma philosophy in the company. As the success of lean six sigma will determine whether their company's profitability will enhance or not. Process owners take over the process after necessary improvements are finalized and applied in the process and they maintain the control phase of the DMAIC cycle.

TEAM MEMBERS

The six sigma transformational process rests on the efforts of the team members involved in it. The team members collect relevant data and define various parameters that need to be improved. They also help the green or black belts with the execution and implementation of the lean six sigma techniques and tools.

CONDITIONS FOR LEAN SIX SIGMA

Certain conditions should be met for the successful application of lean six sigma in a process. The conditions are of varying importance and some might be overlooked while assessing the suitability of the process for applying lean six sigma. Some of the conditions are shared with you in the entailing paragraphs.

THE PROBLEM IS RELATED TO SOME BUSINESS OPERATION

If you recall the definition of lean and six sigma, customer is the main focus and driving force behind both of these philosophies. Value, in lean, is determined from the customer's perspective. If some process or action is not worthy of the money of the customer, you have to classify it as a waste or a non-value-add activity no matter how important you think that process is for your organization. Similarly, in six sigma, the upper and lower specification limit is determined by the customer and everything produced out of the scope of that is termed as a defect. So, as you can see that customer is the king in lean six sigma. As it is focused on the customer, it can be said that it can only be applied to problems related to business.

However, this condition can be tweaked a little bit. If you remember, at the very beginning of this book we promised that lean six sigma can be as beneficial for you as for a businessman, no matter if you are a house wife, a student or someone who is performing any other such role which is not directly linked with the business. The basic modification in the thinking process that you will have to do is to approach your problem from a business point of view. For example, if you are a housewife, you can apply lean six sigma in your daily chores by considering your kids and family members as the customers. Now, if you approach the problem from their perspective, such as what action is essential and what is a waste when you are helping them do their homework. If you are a teacher, you can analyze your teaching methodology on the lines of six sigma and become super-efficient in your work ethics and impact on student's lives. In a nutshell, although lean six sigma is focused on business processes, it can be applied successfully on other fields as well to enhance efficiency and capabilities of those fields.

IT IS A CYCLIC AND FREQUENT PROCESS

Lean six sigma requires a lot of time and energy and you definitely don't want to invest so much resources on an operation that does not have to be repeated over and over again. It is simply not financially viable. At the end of the day, all business philosophies focus on one thing and one thing alone, and that is value generation. If a procedure does not enhance the profitability of the business by providing new and better services for the customer or by introducing efficient procedures which makes the production of the commodities faster and cheaper, it is simply useless to invest your resources in it. So it should be analyzed first that does the process on which we are going to apply lean six sigma is repetitive enough so that it can justify the efforts and resources that will be invested in applying lean six sigma to it.

THE PROBLEM IS UNIQUE IN NATURE

There is no need to reinvent the wheel. If there are established standardized procedures for performing certain processes and these standardized procedures do not produce any waste, if you recall we have discussed the seven types of wastes previously, and there is no variations in the product as the outcomes comfortably attain the six sigma level then there is no need of tweaking such smoothly running operations.

Lean six sigma provides us with amazing results if we apply it on processes which are working on traditional techniques and produce significant amount of waste as well as their outcomes have a lot of variations in them. Such systems give us very encouraging results when we apply lean six sigma technique and methodology in them.

Root Cause of the Issues is Undefined

Here again the reason behind this condition is economic viability. If the root cause of the defects and wastes is known then running the famous DMAIC (Define, Measure, Analyze, Improve, Control) cycle. The system can be transformed into a lean and six sigma system just by addressing that root cause. This way, a lot of time and resources are saved. Business is all about doing the maximum by investing the minimum, lean six sigma is just a means of achieving it. If maximum value generation can be done without applying the philosophy, so be it.

DATA AVAILABILITY

This is perhaps the most important condition for the successful application of the lean six sigma philosophy in a process. Lean as well as six sigma are both data driven approaches. All tools of lean six sigma require some kind of data for their implementation. Data, we can say that, is the backbone of lean six sigma in which the whole philosophy depends on to stand erect. If you have got preexisting data for various steps then it is the best thing for the philosophy's application in the businesses, otherwise special teams have to be formed for the accurate data collection so that baseline performances, key performance indicators and value stream map can be developed. All of these steps are based on solid data and there is no way that without reliable data, lean six sigma can be applied successfully in any business whatsoever.

APPLICATION OF LEAN SIX SIGMA

As promised at the very beginning of this book, when you are finished reading it you will be able to apply lean six sigma not only in business but in everyday chores even if you are a house wife or a student. You are now equipped with the basic concepts as well as tools of lean six sigma, it is time that we discuss it in terms of a practical example.

Let us consider an example of a very compassionate and hardworking housewife. Let us assume that her name is Jessica. She loves to take care of her family but every now and then some blunder happens which destroys her efforts and forces her family to compensate for her short comings. The family does not mind the mistakes as they love Jessica so much but she is driven to remove any shortcomings from her behalf. Finally, Jessica comes across the philosophy of lean six sigma and she decides that it is a perfect methodology which can make her work seamlessly perfect and she must implement it in her daily chores.

Jessica brings all her family and a couple of friends who were expert in dealing with matters pertinent to home maintenance and starts working on the most important DMAIC cycle.

At the very first step, Jessica clearly defines role of each individual. Her husband would assume the role of sponsor as well as champion, he will provide with the necessary materials and financial assistance required for transforming the processes Jessica chose to work on and he will also spearhead and apply those changes, whether it be kitchen redesigning or changing the room furnishing, Jessica's husband will deal with all of it.

The role of green and black belt will be taken up by Jessica's friends who are expert in the relevant processes. Whereas the children will be the team members who will collect relevant data so that value stream map and key performance indicators may be developed. And Jessica will be the process owner who will ultimately take over the system when improvements are finalized. All the family members will be considered as customers whose perspective will be kept in mind when any procedure is to be classified as essential or a waste and their demands will define what outcome will be considered as defected or not.

Now that all roles are finalized, various processes will be chosen for applying lean six sigma in them. For this, it is noted that whether or not relevant of those processes can be collected or not and whether those processes occur frequently or not. After detailed discussion, the family finalized a few of the processes which need improvement but for now, they focused to work on the cooking process only.

Once every parameter was defined, it was time for the measurements. For this purpose a whole month was reserved. Every team member had to note how many times the food which was cooked was faulty or not. The key parameters which were noted were whether the food was served on time, whether it was over cooked or under cooked, whether it was extra salty or bland. Rigorous data collection for the whole month continued when it was decided that the family has got enough measurements and they can accurately draw value stream map and as well as ascertain various key performance indicators.

As you know, the next step after measurements in the DMAIC cycle is analyze. This is the step where the various tools of lean and six sigma come into play. Such as the Why-Why-Why diagram which is extremely helpful in reaching the root cause of errors and variations. Also, the Pareto diagram helps immensely in sorting the various problems in decreasing order of occurrence, this provides a sense of importance and Jessica and her friends used these tools to the full extent. With the help of these tools, they realized that although Jessica knew her recipes well, it was the way things were placed in the kitchen that adversely affected her cooking. For instance, with the help of Why-Why-

Why diagram they were able to understand that the basic reason behind the varying amounts of salt that Jessica used to put in her dishes was because she had different sizes of spoons in the jars of salt and other spices every day which made it difficult for her to measure the exact amount of salt she was pouring in her dishes. The issue of over and under cooking had the basis in the fact that various spices were placed at different locations from the stove. So, if the spices she had to pour in the dish she was cooking on a particular day would be poured instantly while the spices which were placed at the far corner of the kitchen took their time to be found out and hence the dish became overcooked. The Pareto diagram dictated that the issue of salty or bland food preparation was more common as compared to the over and under cooking and hence the salt issue had to sorted out first.

After analyzing the situation with the help of various tools, it was time to improve the system, the 5S tool of lean philosophy came in quite handy in this regard. The various cutlery present in the kitchen was sorted out according to its size and use and then the cutlery was set in order of increasing size and the most frequently used cutlery was placed nearest to the hearth and clear labels stating the size and name of certain utensil which was present in the particular box was glued on the box. Mistake proofing was done by using different colored boxes for each kind of utensil. After everything thing was set so that the reasons behind varying levels of salt was covered, the kitchen was readjusted so that all utensils and spices were placed as near as possible to the hearth so that the waste which was occurring because of unnecessary motion could be avoided.

After the improvement cycle was over, the kitchen was handed over to Jessica who kept a close look on the occurrence of problems and told the team members, the children, to note all the problems and their frequency.

Jessica was ecstatic when she realized that after many months, thanks to lean six sigma, no issues related to cooking ever occurred and she was happy to realize that it was not her fault rather the process needed some tweaks. After the successful application of lean six sigma in cooking Jessica was really interested in applying the philosophy of lean six sigma in other fields of her life as well and we are sure that after reading this book you will also benefit from this amazing methodology.

Do not go yet; One last thing to do

If you enjoyed this book or found it useful I'd be very grateful if you'd post a short review on **Amazon***. Your support really does make a difference and I read all the reviews personally so I can get your feedback and make this book even better.*

Thanks again for your support!

CPSIA information can be obtained
at www.ICGtesting.com
Printed in the USA
BVHW040252280421
605952BV00015B/2141